MATERIALS ALL AROUND US

CHANGING MATERIALS

Robert Snedden

Heinemann
LIBRARY

www.heinemann.co.uk/library
Visit our website to find out more information about Heinemann Library books.

To order:
☎ Phone 44 (0) 1865 888066
🖹 Send a fax to 44 (0) 1865 314091
💻 Visit the Heinemann Bookshop at www.heinemann.co.uk/library to browse our
catalogue and order online.

First published in Great Britain by Heinemann Library,
Halley Court, Jordan Hill, Oxford OX2 8EJ
a division of Reed Educational and Professional Publishing Ltd.
Heinemann is a registered trademark of Reed Educational & Professional Publishing Ltd.

OXFORD MELBOURNE AUCKLAND
JOHANNESBURG BLANTYRE GABORONE
IBADAN PORTSMOUTH (NH) USA CHICAGO

Designed by Celia Floyd
Originated by Dot Gradations
Printed by Wing King Tong, Hong Kong

ISBN 0 431 12091 9 (hardback)   ISBN 0 431 12096 X (paperback)
05 04 03 02   06 05 04 03 02
10 9 8 7 6 5 4 3 2   10 9 8 7 6 5 4 3 2 1

British Library Cataloguing in Publication Data

Snedden, Robert
   Changing materials. - (Material all around us)
   1.Matter - Properties - Juvenile literature 2.Materials science -
   Juvenile literature
   I.Title
   530.4

Acknowledgements
The Publishers would like to thank the following for permission to reproduce
photographs: Actionplus: P Millereau p5; Andrew Lambert: p18, p26; Environmental
Images: Vanessa Miles p16; Environmental Picture Library: Pete Addis p19, Leslie
Garland pp7, 24; Network: Barry Lewis p21; Sally and Richard Greenhill: p20; Science
Photo Library: Martin Bond p4, Charles D Winters p10, Rosenfeld Images Ltd p11, John
Greim p12; Tony Stone Images: David Hoffman p8, Christopher Bissell p22, Robert Yager
p23, Matthew McVay p29

Cover photograph reproduced with permission of Science Photo Library

Every effort has been made to contact copyright holders of any material reproduced in
this book. Any omissions will be rectified in subsequent printings if notice is given to
the Publisher.

Any words appearing in the text in bold, **like this**, are explained in the glossary.

Contents

A world of change

Many of the materials we use are thrown away after being used for only a short time.

Everything changes with time. Things get broken, batteries go dead, clothes wear out and food goes bad. These materials and all the other materials that we use are acted upon by many outside forces.

The right choice

Some materials, like a paper towel, are designed to be used just once. Others have to last longer. You wouldn't want to buy a new set of clothes everyday, which rules out tissue paper for clothing! When choosing a material it is important to know how and where it will be used.

Changing conditions

The materials we use in the world around us will meet changes in temperature, stresses and pressure depending on the job they have to do. Materials scientists have to know how different materials behave when they meet these changes.

Materials scientists also have to know how a material will react with the other materials it will meet in everyday use. For example, iron has to be protected from rusting by keeping it from contact with the air. Kitchen utensils have to be made from materials that won't react with the foods they are used to prepare. A car battery has to be made of a material that won't be corroded by the acid inside it.

Materials scientists are always looking for new and improved materials. Understanding how they react to change is an important part of that search. A new material will be given a series of tests to make sure that it can perform the job it is needed for.

A glass bicycle might look wonderful, but what would happen the first time it hit a bump?

Chemical reactions

A **chemical reaction** takes place when two or more substances react together to form new substances. For a chemical reaction to take place the **bonds** that hold **atoms** together have to be broken and reformed in a different way.

When two substances react together the bonds that hold the atoms together are broken and reformed to make new substances.

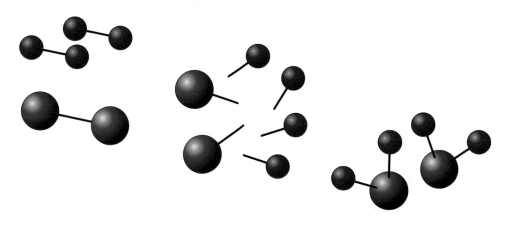

Chemical reactions can be slow, like iron combining with oxygen to form rust, or very fast, like an explosion. Most chemical reactions produce heat, although some need heat to get them started.

Chemical changes

No matter how different the products of a chemical reaction might be from the substances that reacted together to produce them, no matter is lost in a chemical reaction. If you weighed all the substances involved before they reacted together and then weighed all the new substances that had been produced you would find that the weights were the same.

Reactants and products

The substances that react together are called the reactants. When a chemical reaction takes place the new substances produced might look nothing like the chemicals that reacted together. For example, white crystals of common salt are very different from greenish-yellow chlorine gas and soft sodium metal. The substances that are produced are called the products.

sodium (metal) + chlorine (gas) = sodium chloride (common salt – solid)

Chemical reactions are different from the physical changes that can take place in a material. For example, melting is a physical change. The appearance of a substance changes when it melts but it is still the same substance.

If iron is left exposed to the air it will react with oxygen to form iron oxide, or rust. Covering it with a protective coat can help to prevent this happening.

Reaction rates

It is important to know how materials will react before they are brought together. Some can react together very rapidly, releasing a great deal of energy, which could be dangerous.

Before chemicals can react together the **molecules** that make them up have to be on the move so they can collide with each other. If the molecules bang together with enough force the **bonds** holding them together can be broken and new **compounds** can form. The **atoms** in a solid move much less than those in a liquid or a gas. In a reaction such as rusting, which involves a solid, collisions with enough energy don't happen that often and so the iron rusts slowly.

An explosion takes place as a result of a very rapid and highly energetic chemical reaction.

Changing the rate

The rate of a reaction can be changed in different ways. Heating the chemicals makes the molecules move faster and so increases the chances of collisions taking place. Cooling slows down the movement of the molecules, cutting down on the collisions. This is why freezing food is a good way of preventing it from going bad.

The size of the **particles** involved in the reaction is also important. Chopping something up very finely will make it react faster. A large lump of coal will burn fairly slowly and steadily but the same amount of coal ground up to form coal dust will explode violently if it is blown into a flame.

Try it yourself

You will need
sand
water
vinegar
bicarbonate of soda
red food-colouring
large dish
small plastic bottle

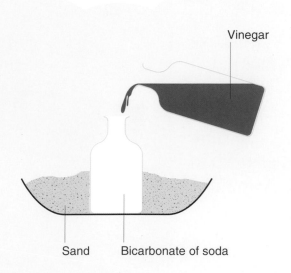

1 Add some food colouring to the vinegar.

2 Fill the bottle halfway up with water and dissolve a couple of teaspoons of bicarbonate of soda in it.

3 Pile sand around the bottle to make a volcano cone, leaving the top of the bottle uncovered. Now pour the red vinegar into the bottle and watch your volcano erupt!

Metal reactions

Metals can be ordered in a series that is a little like a league table for metals. The most reactive metal is at the top of the table and the least reactive at the bottom. Unlike, say, a football league table there are never any upsets in the **reactivity series**. Metals at the top will always react more strongly than metals at the bottom. Some metals, such as potassium, are so highly reactive that they are never found on their own in nature but always as part of a **compound** with other materials. Gold is highly valued because it does not react very easily with other materials and so looks as good as new even after hundreds of years.

Potassium is such a highly reactive metal that it is never found as a pure element in nature.

Steel is often coated in a thin layer of zinc to prevent rusting. This is called galvanisation. Zinc is more reactive than iron and will more readily combine with oxygen.

Displacement

The higher a metal is in the reactivity series, the more stable are the compounds that it forms, and so the more difficult it is to extract the pure metal. In displacement reactions a less reactive **element** is replaced in a compound by a more reactive one. For example, if powdered zinc is added to a solution of copper sulphate the zinc displaces the copper metal and forms zinc sulphate. This is because zinc is more reactive than the copper.

Aluminium

Aluminium is actually a highly reactive metal. Until a way was found of extracting it cheaply it was so difficult to obtain that it was more highly valued than gold. The metal naturally forms a surface coating of unreactive aluminium oxide that prevents the metal beneath from corroding. This is what makes it so useful.

11

Oxidation and reduction

A breathalyser is used by police to determine how much alcohol someone has consumed. Alcohol causes an oxidation reaction to take place that makes a chemical in the breathalyser change colour.

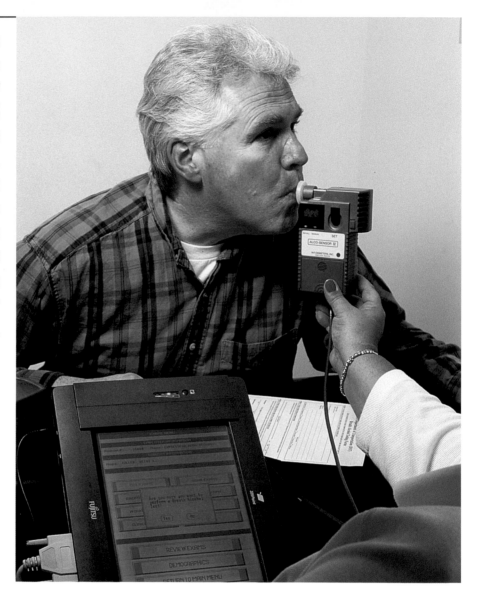

Oxidation is a **chemical reaction** in which a substance combines with oxygen. When you burn something oxidation is taking place very rapidly. When iron rusts oxidation is taking place slowly as the iron combines with oxygen from the air. Inside your body the food you eat is combined with the air you breathe to produce carbon dioxide, water and energy. This is another example of oxidation.

Redox reactions

Reduction is the opposite of oxidation. It happens when a substance loses oxygen. When iron **ore**, a **compound** of iron and oxygen, is heated with carbon the carbon removes the oxygen from the iron ore, leaving iron behind. The iron has been reduced. The carbon is oxidized in the process, becoming carbon dioxide gas.

Oxidation and reduction always happen together in a balanced reaction, called a **redox reaction**. Reduction can also be used to describe any chemical reaction in which a substance combines with hydrogen.

Combustion

Combustion is a very rapid oxidation reaction, producing energy in the form of heat and light. This energy is called the heat of combustion. The lowest temperature at which a solid or liquid will catch fire is called its ignition temperature. Once the reaction has started the heat of combustion will keep it going.

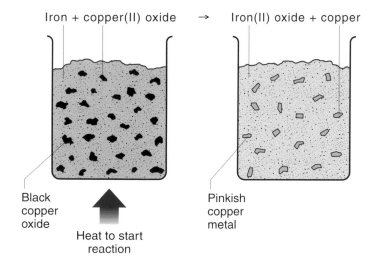

Iron + copper(II) oxide → Iron(II) oxide + copper

Black copper oxide

Heat to start reaction

Pinkish copper metal

When powdered iron is heated with copper oxide the copper oxide is reduced to copper metal and the iron is oxidised to iron oxide.

Catalysts

Catalysts are substances that can change the rate of a **chemical reaction**, or make the reaction possible, without being changed themselves. They are used in many manufacturing processes, speeding up chemical reactions that otherwise would take place too slowly to be practical.

Zeolites are catalysts that have a honeycomb structure that traps molecules while they react with each other. Zeolites can be made with different sized holes to suit different reactions.

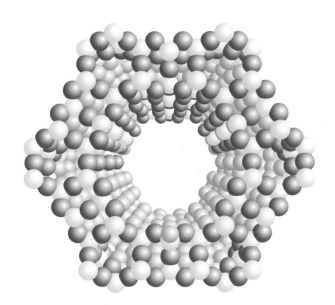

Hydrogenation

Hydrogenation is a chemical process in which hydrogen is added to a substance. Vegetable oils are often hydrogenated to produce solid fats such as margarines and low-fat butter substitutes. Catalysts are needed to make hydrogenation economical. Nickel metal is a good hydrogenation catalyst.

How catalysts work

All chemical reactions need energy to get them started. This is called the **activation energy**. Catalysts work by changing the activation energy for a reaction. They do this by providing a new way for the reaction to take place. When the activation energy level is lowered, the reaction rate is increased and the reaction is said to be catalyzed.

If the activation energy level is raised, the reaction rate decreases and the reaction is said to be inhibited.

Some substances, called promoters, increase the activity of a catalyst. Other substances can reduce the effects of a catalyst. These are called poisons.

Enzymes: natural catalysts

Catalysts make life possible. Most of the chemical reactions that take place in living things are ones that have high activation energies. By themselves, they would take place slowly, if at all. These reactions are speeded up by natural catalysts called **enzymes**. Some enzymes actually make reactions happen a billion times faster than they would do normally. Without a catalyst it would take weeks to convert starch into glucose, for example. You'd starve to death waiting for it to happen. Just a tiny amount of the enzyme ptyalin, found in saliva, speeds up the reaction so that starches can be digested and used to provide energy for your body.

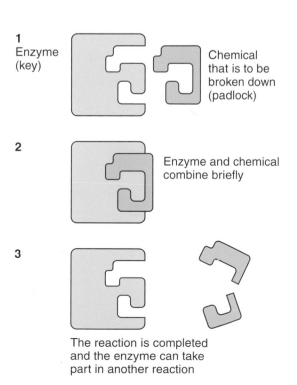

1
Enzyme
(key)

Chemical
that is to be
broken down
(padlock)

2

Enzyme and chemical
combine briefly

3

The reaction is completed
and the enzyme can take
part in another reaction

Enzymes work by a 'lock and key' mechanism where reacting chemicals combine on the surface of the enzyme.

Acids

Acids are found in all sorts of places – in fizzy drinks, in car batteries, even in our stomachs. Acids are used in the production of food and drinks and to kill bacteria in food. Many acids are poisonous and strong acids such as sulphuric acid are highly corrosive, which means that they can burn clothes or skin. Acids in rain can damage buildings and kill trees. The chemical industry produces 150 million tonnes of sulphuric acid a year – it is an essential part of the production of fertilizers, paints, detergents and other materials.

Acid properties

All acids have properties in common. **Solutions** of acids have a sour taste and produce a burning sensation if they come into contact with the skin.

Acid rain causes a great deal of damage to stone. Some carvings that had lasted for hundreds of years have been severely eroded.

Acids can dissolve many metals. **Litmus** is a dye that is used to test whether liquids are acid or **alkaline**. Blue litmus paper will turn red if it is brought into contact with acid.

Substances can be ranked on a pH scale, which indicates how acid or how alkaline they are. The most acid substances have a pH of 0, the most alkaline have a pH of 14.

Organic and inorganic acids

Organic acids are always carbon **compounds**. They are used in drinks, cosmetics, food and soaps. The first known acid was vinegar, an organic acid. Common organic acids include citric acid, which is found in citrus fruits and vitamin C.

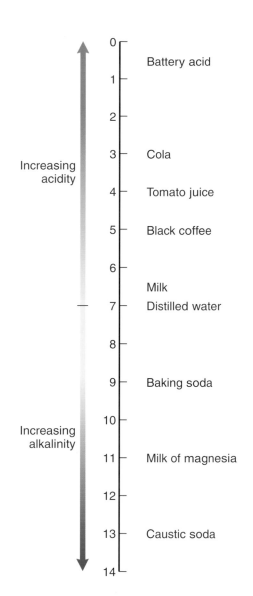

Increasing acidity

0
1
2
3 — Cola
4 — Tomato juice
5 — Black coffee
6
7 — Milk / Distilled water
8
9 — Baking soda
10

Increasing alkalinity

11 — Milk of magnesia
12
13 — Caustic soda
14

0 — Battery acid

Some common materials and their pHs.

Generally speaking, inorganic acids do not contain carbon. Many inorganic acids are strong and can be highly corrosive. They are used in the production of other chemicals and in the refining of crude oil. Sulphuric acid, a strong inorganic acid, is commonly used in car batteries.

Alkalis

Millions of tonnes of **alkali** are produced every year by the chemical industry. Many household oven cleaners contain the alkali sodium hydroxide, which can break down the deposits of fat that build up on the walls of ovens. Potassium hydroxide, also called caustic potash, is boiled with vegetable oils or animal fats to make soft soaps that dissolve easily in water. Magnesium hydroxide is often used as an ingredient in antacids, which are used to treat indigestion caused by excess stomach acidity.

Alkali properties

Strong alkalis are just as corrosive as strong **acids** and can cause serious burns. Alkalis in **solution** are soapy, or slippery, to the touch and have a bitter taste. Red **litmus** paper turns blue if it is brought into contact with an alkali.

A wasp sting hurts because it contains an alkali. The effect of the sting can be neutralised by applying a weak acid such as vinegar.

Oven cleaners use strong alkalis like sodium hydroxide to break down fatty deposits.

A soil that is too acidic will lose essential nutrients so farmers spread the alkali calcium hydroxide (powdered lime).

Neutralization

Whenever an acid and an alkali react together they produce a salt plus water – this process is called neutralization. For example, hydrochloric acid and sodium hydroxide give common salt (sodium chloride) and water when they are mixed together.

Try it yourself

You will need
red cabbage, chopped   large jar
knife   chopping board
saucepan   sieve
half litre of distilled water

1 Boil the distilled water in a saucepan.
2 Remove from the heat and add the chopped cabbage. Leave until cool.
3 Strain the purple-red liquid into a jar.

You can use this liquid as an indicator to test whether substances are acid or alkaline. Acids will turn the indicator red, while alkalis will turn it green. To test a substance pour a little of the indicator into a small jar and then add a drop of the substance you are testing. Try lemon juice and vinegar which are weak acids, and milk of magnesia and baking soda which are alkalis.

Warning: Do NOT attempt to test strong alkalis such as oven cleaners or strong acids.

Physical changes

Materials are affected by physical changes in temperature, in pressure and by bending and stretching and other forces.

The physical properties of different materials allow them to be used for different purposes. Glass is very brittle, but it is useful because it is transparent and can be shaped easily when it is molten.

Plastics are lightweight and waterproof and can be moulded into any shape, so they are excellent for making containers.

Metals are tough and strong, easily shaped into thin wires or into sheets. They are good conductors of electricity and heat. They are also highly reflective when polished. Metals are very useful materials indeed.

Ice cream only stays semi-solid while it is cold. On a hot day it will soon melt and drip if you don't eat it quickly!

Solutions

Many substances can be dissolved in water, or some other liquids, to form a **solution**. Salt can be dissolved in water to give a liquid solution of salt and water, for example. Dissolving a substance is a physical change, not a chemical one. If the water is removed by evaporation a solid deposit of salt will be left behind.

If a solution of salt in water is allowed to evaporate deposits of salt crystals are **left behind**.

Try it yourself

You will need
a shallow dish
a beaker
some warm water
table salt

1 Pour the water into the beaker and add salt, stirring until it has dissolved.
2 Pour some of the salt solution into a shallow dish and leave it in a warm place until the water has evaporated.

You will see the salt crystals that have been left behind. Taste a little to prove to yourself that the salt has not been changed by dissolving in the water.

Stresses and strains

Sometimes materials are acted on by forces that may make the material change shape because it isn't able to move. A force acting on a material is a stress, and strain is the amount by which the material changes shape as a result of that force. Some materials, such as rubber, can change shape readily. Others, such as concrete, do not.

An archer pulling back a bow is putting stress on the bow and bowstring. When the string is released they will spring back to their original shape.

If you put too much stress on a material that cannot change shape, it will give way.

Elasticity

The ability of an object to return to its original size and shape, after being pushed or pulled by a force is called **elasticity**. All solids have some elasticity. A rubber band is very elastic, whereas a brick is not.

No matter how elastic a material is, if the stress is great enough it will no longer return to its original shape after the force is removed. When this happens the material is said to have passed its elastic limit.

Elastic energy

When you compress a spring you are transferring energy into the spring. The energy you are storing there is called elastic potential energy. As soon as the spring can return to its original shape this energy will be released. Buildings in earthquake zones are often built on giant springs that can absorb the energy of an earthquake. Building materials like concrete are very inelastic and the forces produced by an earthquake soon push them past their elastic limit, shattering them.

Concrete structures do not have a great deal of elasticity. The stress of an earthquake can cause them to break and collapse.

Heat

Materials are exposed to heat in many ways. We use heat to cook our food and to warm our homes. Heat is used to refine crude oil and to separate metals from their **ores**. It can be used to melt materials so that we can reshape them. Changes in temperature can have many effects on materials. Heating can make materials expand, melt, boil and **evaporate**, while cooling makes them **contract**, **condense** and freeze.

Heat flows

If something that is hot comes into contact with something that is cold heat passes from the hot object to the cold object until the temperature of both is the same. If you step into a hot bath, energy is transferred to your cooler body, making you feel warm. However, if you step into a cold bath heat will flow from you to the bathwater, making you feel rather chilly!

Railway engineers were aware that metals expanded on hot days, so rail tracks were laid with gaps to allow for this.

Expanding and contracting

When heat flows into a material the **atoms** move more rapidly and take up more space, so the substance expands. When heat flows out the atoms, or **molecules**, move more slowly and the material contracts.

Moving heat

Heat moves through a material by **conduction**. If a metal rod is heated at one end atoms in the hot end begin to move faster and strike nearby atoms. These atoms then strike atoms further along the rod. In this way, the heat travels through the metal. If the heated metal rod heats the air around it the heated air expands and rises and cooler air replaces it. The cooler air that is now near the rod becomes warm and rises in its turn. This flow of heated air moving away from a hot object and cooler air flowing towards it is called a **convection current**.

Insulating materials

Heat does not travel easily through some materials, such as plastic and wood. These materials are called insulators. This is why many cooking utensils have plastic or wood handles to protect your hand from the heat.

Stopper

Liquid

Vacuum

A vacuum flask has a vacuum held between two layers to prevent heat being conducted in or out.

Pressure

Pressure is a force acting on a surface. A force concentrated on a small area produces a greater pressure than the same force acting over a large area. Pressure is important in the behaviour of gases. If a gas in a container gets hot, for example, the pressure increases and the container might explode.

Blowing up a balloon makes the pressure on the inside greater than the air pressure outside.

Aircraft flying high up where the air pressure is very low, and submarines beneath the sea where the pressure of the water is very high, have to be built from materials that can cope with these extremes.

If a gas is put under pressure its **volume** gets smaller. This happens because the gas **molecules** are pushed closer together. This is used in car tyres.

Gas-filled car tyres absorb the shock of going over bumps in the road as the gas is compressed by the force of the bump and then expands again.

Air pressure

There is so much air in the atmosphere above us that it presses on us with a pressure of about 1.1 kilograms per square centimetre. The total air pressure on your body probably amounts to thousands of kilograms. The reason you are not aware of this huge force is because the fluid and air in your body pushes out with an equal, balancing pressure.

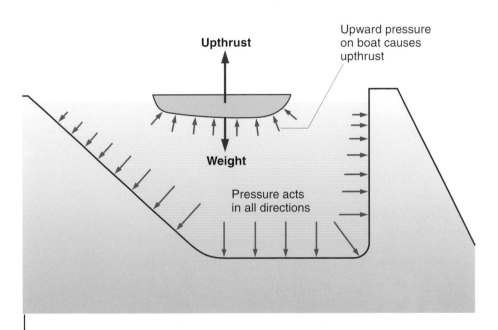

Upthrust

Upward pressure on boat causes upthrust

Weight

Pressure acts in all directions

A liquid exerts pressure evenly in all directions and keeps the boat afloat.

Radioactivity

Some materials are made of **atoms** that are unstable and break up over time. Materials that do this are said to be **radioactive**. As they break up these atoms produce energy that can be put to use in nuclear power stations, in batteries for pacemakers and power cells for space probes.

What is radioactivity?

Atoms are made up of clouds of **electrons** surrounding a heavier **nucleus**. Radioactive substances, such as the elements radium, uranium and plutonium have unstable nuclei. They release radiation in the form of atomic particles, changing into different forms of the same element or into other elements as they do so until finally they become stable and nonradioactive.

In the course of a lengthy many-step process radioactive uranium eventually becomes stable.

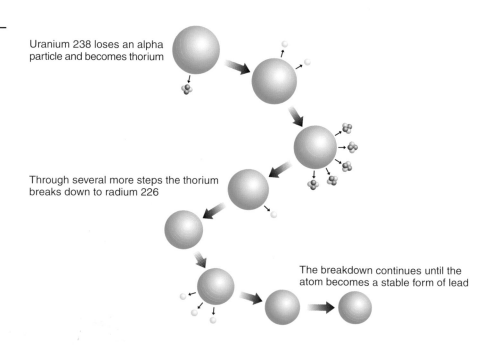

Uranium 238 loses an alpha particle and becomes thorium

Through several more steps the thorium breaks down to radium 226

The breakdown continues until the atom becomes a stable form of lead

Particle radiation

A radioactive **element** can give off radiation in different ways. Alpha particles are fast-moving particles that are identical to the nuclei of helium atoms. They do not travel far and can be stopped by a sheet of paper. Beta particles are electrons. They are also fast moving and can be stopped by a sheet of metal. Gamma rays are not particles but a form of high energy electromagnetic radiation. It takes a thick sheet of lead to stop them.

Uranium, the fuel used in a nuclear reactor, gives off particles called neutrons as it breaks down. These strike other uranium atoms making them break apart too, which releases more neutrons. This is a chain reaction.

The problem of what to do with dangerous nuclear waste has never been satisfactorily solved.

Glossary

acid a corrosive, sour tasting substance that turns blue litmus red and will neutralize an alkali

activation energy the amount of energy needed for a chemical reaction to begin

alkali a corrosive, slippery or soapy compound that turns red litmus blue and will neutralize an acid

atom tiny particle from which all materials are made; smallest part of an element that exists

bonds forces that hold atoms together in molecules

catalyst a substance that alters the rate of a chemical reaction without itself being changed

chemical reaction a reaction that takes place between two or more substances in which energy is given out or taken in and new substances are produced

combustion the rapid combination of a substance with oxygen, in other words burning

compound a substance that is made up of atoms of two or more elements

condense to change from a gas into a liquid

conduction movement of heat through a solid from an area of high temperature to an area of lower temperature

contract to get smaller

convection current the movement of heat through a liquid or gas caused by the tendency of warmer material to rise through colder material

elasticity the ability of a solid to return to its original shape once distorting forces have been removed

electrons negatively-charged particles that are found in all atoms; the main carriers of electrical energy

element a substance that cannot be broken down into simpler substances by chemical reactions; an element is made up of just one type of atom

enzyme a natural catalyst that regulates the rate of a chemical activity in a living organism

evaporate change into a vapour or a gas

litmus an indicator used to tell whether something is acid or alkaline; litmus turns red in the presence of acid, blue in the presence of alkali

molecule two or more atoms combined together; if the atoms are the same it is an element, if they are different it is a compound

neutron one of the fundamental components of an atom, found in the atom's nucleus; a neutron has no electric charge

nucleus the heavy, central part of an atom, made up of protons and neutrons

ore rock from which metals can be obtained

oxidation a chemical reaction in which oxygen combines with a substance

radioactive elements that emit high energy rays and particles

raw material material in its natural state

reactivity series a list of elements ordered by how easily they react with other elements

redox reaction reduction and oxidation occurring together in a reaction

reduction a chemical reaction in which a substance loses oxygen

soluble able to be dissolved

solution a mixture of one substance dissolved in another

vapour a type of gas

volume the amount of space occupied by something

Index